MONEY MANAGEMENT FOR KIDS

Simplest ways to teach kids on money management

Copyright©2021 Mary Peterson

All Rights Reserved

TABLE OF CONTENT

Table of Contents

INTRODUCTION 4

CHAPTER ONE 6

   KIDS AND MONEY – THE FIRST LESSON 6

CHAPTER TWO 10

   Ways to Show Children Monetary Obligation 10

CHAPTER THREE 16

   Showing Kids How to Budget 16

CHAPTER FOUR 24

   15   Tips to Show Your Youngster on how to save money 24

CHAPTER FIVE 38

     CONCLUSION 38

INTRODUCTION

You need your kid(s) to be gifted at dealing with their own money as they grow up and you may be concern on how best to teach them about money.

Children structure their money tendency from about seven years of age, and that their attentive eyeballs are typically watching when their folks make money related exchanges. With a smidgen of intentional participation, you can give your children a monetary head start.

Start by assisting kids with noticing and calculating the trading of money from a tender age and by requesting their assessment when you're preparing to make a purchase, which could be enormous or little.

CHAPTER ONE

KIDS AND MONEY – THE FIRST LESSON

At the point when you're showing your children money, it's imperative to encourage them to know where the money comes from. Money doesn't simply come from guardians and kin, however when you work, you get paid or when you offer service to individuals, you likewise get paid.

The key is to continually exhibit and explain the connection among work and money.

Show the three fundamental standards of money: giving, saving and spending.

Giving is perhaps the most significant of the three classifications since you're instructing them to feel the effect of helping other people at a youthful age. That is priceless. With respect to saving and spending, urge your kid to put to the side a portion of their money to investment funds and some to investing every energy they get paid. Advise them that once their money is gone, it's gone. Furthermore, indeed, your children will commit errors, yet its better that they commit those errors under the wellbeing of your rooftop.

CHAPTER TWO

Ways to Show Children Monetary Obligation

1. **Take your youngster shopping for food** - Take your children to the supermarket and work the spending plan with their information. It is advisable to do this with more modest decisions with your little children and in a greater manner with your older kid.

2. **Give them genuine money to oversee** - Nothing beats genuine exercises. Start with basic exercises and shopping trips. Make your children handle money and tally change. So they know how – as well as so they look and feel certain doing it. A model: Christmas shopping for family members. Set the sum and perceive how they work it out. It is ok to make ideas however permit them to settle on decisions.

3. **Teach the Save, Spend, Give ideal** - This is the fundamental decision we as a whole make with each dollar we procure. In

more seasoned children, it is suitable to do this in financial balances and with spending plans. In little youngsters, we like having 3 named, obvious containers where every kid can make a choice with the money they acquire and see the outcome. Try to show all children to put something aside for a target objective – an exceptional toy or a vehicle, instruct them to put something aside for an objective that feels far away.

4. **Matching their reserve funds and clarify why you are doing it and how you are capable -** On the off chance that you

are in a situation to do so consider coordinating with what the money your children have endeavored to put something aside for school, prom or a vehicle and so forth... Disclose to them why you are coordinating with their investment funds.

5. **Teach them the advantages and prizes of covering the bills on schedule -** This is a brilliant rule. This training can introduce the chance to talk great credit and awful credit. This is a significant exercise for more established children particularly.

6. **Teach them about offering monetarily to an association or cause -** Indeed, show them the component of monetary duty that is offering in return.

7. **Create and empower a youthful business visionary -** Succeeding and coming up short in little manners with money will assist kids with seeing how to apply those exercises for a bigger scope.

CHAPTER THREE

Showing Kids How to Budget

Showing youngsters how to have a financial plan at a youthful age will be useful for them sometime down the road. At the point when your kid gets money as an allowance or as a financial gift, you can help kick them off with straightforward planning ideas.

Start With Objectives, Wants and Needs

Talk with your kid about money and how to utilize it shrewdly. Discussion about their objectives for their money. What do they want? What do they need? There might be momentary objectives they can be bought immediately. They may have long term objectives that will expect them to save over a long period. It is useful for youngsters to have a token of why they are saving and why they ought not to go through the entirety of their money now.

Save, Share and Spend Strategy

Save, Share and Spend is a technique for kids where they put to the side money toward every one of these three things.

Save

At the point when your youngster brings in money, they should initially save a bit for reserve funds. The proposal is to save at any rate 10% of income. This rate can be expanded for youngsters since they have less costs. Reserve funds can be amassed from numerous points of view. Some utilization a container, piggybank or even a joint ledger to acquire revenue. The bank account ought to be saved for crises (new bicycle tire) just as longer-term objectives (first vehicle).

Share

Training youngsters about foundation at a youthful age is additionally helpful. Permit them to research and add to a foundation of their decision. Sharing is regularly around 10%. Talk about choices with your kid to figure out which course they may appreciate making a difference. Additionally consider having them volunteer with that association to perceive what they are really making a difference. For instance, it tends to be remunerating for youngsters to utilize money to buy toys for a neighborhood outreach focus. At that point they can assist to give out those items to the needy people at Christmas.

Spend

The rest of their income can go toward spending. The spending type is open so your kid can make purchases of goods they pick, however advise them that extra savings will help them arrive at their drawn out objectives quicker.

Start Little, and Set a Model

It is useful for your kids to perceive how you budget, yet start little. For instance, permit them to help you plan the week after week shopping for food. Start by arranging a rundown from deal flyers and coupons, and afterward adhere to that rundown at the store. This can transform into a saving game for them. Keep in mind, kids will gain from your model. So educating them concerning planning is significant, however it's considerably more effective in the event that they see you following a spending yourself.

CHAPTER FOUR

15   Tips to Show Your Youngster on how to save money

1.   Introduce the Idea of Money

Acquaint small children with coins first. Show them the estimation of coins and urge them to save their coins in a stash. Utilize a reasonable stash or container so that children can really see their heap of money develop.

2. Talk about Wants versus Needs

The initial phase in showing kids the benefit of saving is to assist them with separating wants and needs. Clarify that needs incorporate the essentials, like food, cover, fundamental dress, medical care, and instruction. Wants are for the most part the additional items—from film tickets and candy to planner shoes, a bike or the most recent cell phone. You can utilize your own budget as an illustration to delineate how wants should take a rearward sitting arrangement to needs as far as spending.

3. Let Them Bring in Their Own Money

In the event that you need your kids to become savers, permit them to bring in and set aside money and give them the chance to figure out how to utilize it. At the point when you offer allowances in return for tasks, they're additionally learning the value of their diligent effort.

4. Set Savings Objectives

To a child, being advised to save—without clarifying why—may appear to be futile. Assisting kids to outline a saving objective can be a superior method to get them roused. In the event that they understand what it is they need to put something aside for, help them separate their objectives into reasonable nibbles. On the off chance that they need to purchase a $50 computer game, for instance, and they get a $10 recompense every week, help them sort out how long it will take for them to arrive at that objective, in light of their investment funds rate.

5. **Give a place to Save**

When your kids have a savings objective as a main priority, they'll need a spot to stash their money. For more youthful children, this might be a stash, yet in the event that they're somewhat more established, you might need to set them up with their own checking or investment account at a bank. That way they can perceive how their investment funds are adding up and how much advancement they're making toward their objective.

6. Have Them Track Spending

Part of being a superior saver implies knowing where your money is going. In the event that your kids get a stipend, having them record their purchases every day and add them up toward the week's end can be an enlightening encounter. Urge them to consider how they're spending and how much quicker they could arrive at their reserve funds objective if they somehow managed to change their spending designs.

7. **Offer Savings Motivations**

One reason individuals save in their boss' retirement plan is the organization coordinating with commitment. All things considered, who doesn't care with the expectation of complimentary money? In case you're experiencing difficulty rousing your children to save, you can go through that equivalent rule to incline their endeavors. In the event that your youngster has define a major investment funds objective—for instance, a $400 tablet—you could offer to coordinate with a level of what they have saved. As another option, you could offer an award when your child arrives at an investment funds achievement, for example, a $50 reward for hitting the midway imprint.

8. Leave Space for Errors

Some portion of placing kids in charge of their own money is allowing them to gain from their mistakes. It's enticing to step in and steer kids from a conceivably exorbitant mix-up, however it very well might be smarter to utilize that botch as a workable second. That way they'll know later on how not to manage their money.

9. Go about as Their Loan boss

One of the fundamental precepts of saving is to not maintain an unsustainable lifestyle. On the off chance that your youngster has something they need to purchase and is being fretful about putting something aside for it, turning into your child's leaser can assist with showing an important exercise saving. Say your youngster needs to buy something that costs $100. You could loan the money and require installment from the stipend you give, with premium. The exercise you need to instruct is that saving may mean deferring satisfaction longer, yet the thing you need to purchase will wind up costing less on the off chance that you stand by.

10. Discussion about Money

On the off chance that you need children to find out about saving, it should be a continuous conversation. Regardless of whether you plan a customary week by week registration to discuss money or bring in money talks a piece of your day by day round, the key is to make a big difference for the discussion.

11. **Set a Genuine Example**

In the event that you need your youngsters to become savers, being one yourself can help. Getting your secret stash fit as a fiddle, opening a bank account, or basically expanding your arrangement commitments are all means that you can require to support saving as a family movement. You could likewise choose to put something aside for something together, like an extra-large flat screen television, a family get-away, or a pool.

12. Present Long term Forecasting

Show your children about long term money savings and liability. Talk about different expenses they could use their long term savings to acquire – houses, holiday, cars to mention a few.

13. Teach About Financing

Whenever they've dominated fundamental financial abilities, urge your children to find out about the intricacy of globalized markets. Investigate stocks, shared assets, or bank accounts.

14. Instruct Children to Set Objectives

Numerous effective monetary achievements are accomplished by objective setting. Urge your children to set money savings objectives and work towards them.

15. Make Learning Fun

Play money games that support learning. Tabletop games, web based games, and natively constructed games are generally potential outcomes.

CHAPTER FIVE

CONCLUSION

Encourage kids to save by teaching them about savings all through the year. As a parent, you need to make savings a regular life style of your kids in order for them to have a solid foundation for a great financial future.

Kids that have great training on money management early in life are sure to always have money and never be broke or have empty wallets.

www.ingramcontent.com/pod-product-compliance
Lightning Source LLC
Chambersburg PA
CBHW050322220526

45465CB00005B/2091